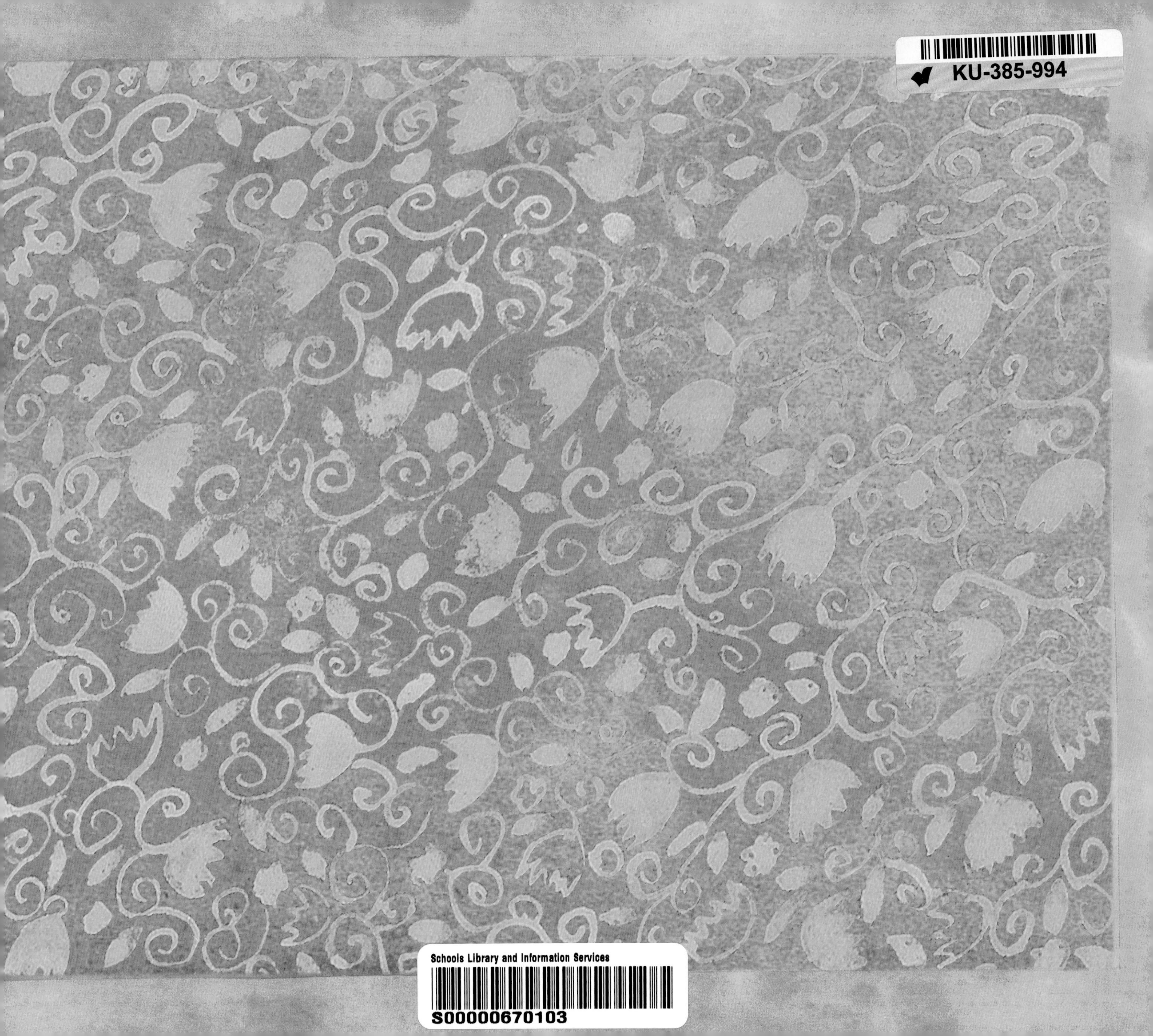

اسلامی فنون کا تصوّراتی سفر

Journey through Islamic Art

Na'ima bint Robert & Diana Mayo

mantra

میں نے بغداد اور سمرقند کے شہروں، ہندوستان میں مغلوں اور
اسپین میں عرب نژاد مسلمانوں کے متعلق بہت قصّے سُنے تھے۔

I heard tales about the cities of Samarkand and Baghdad,
About the Moghuls in India and the Moors in Spain.

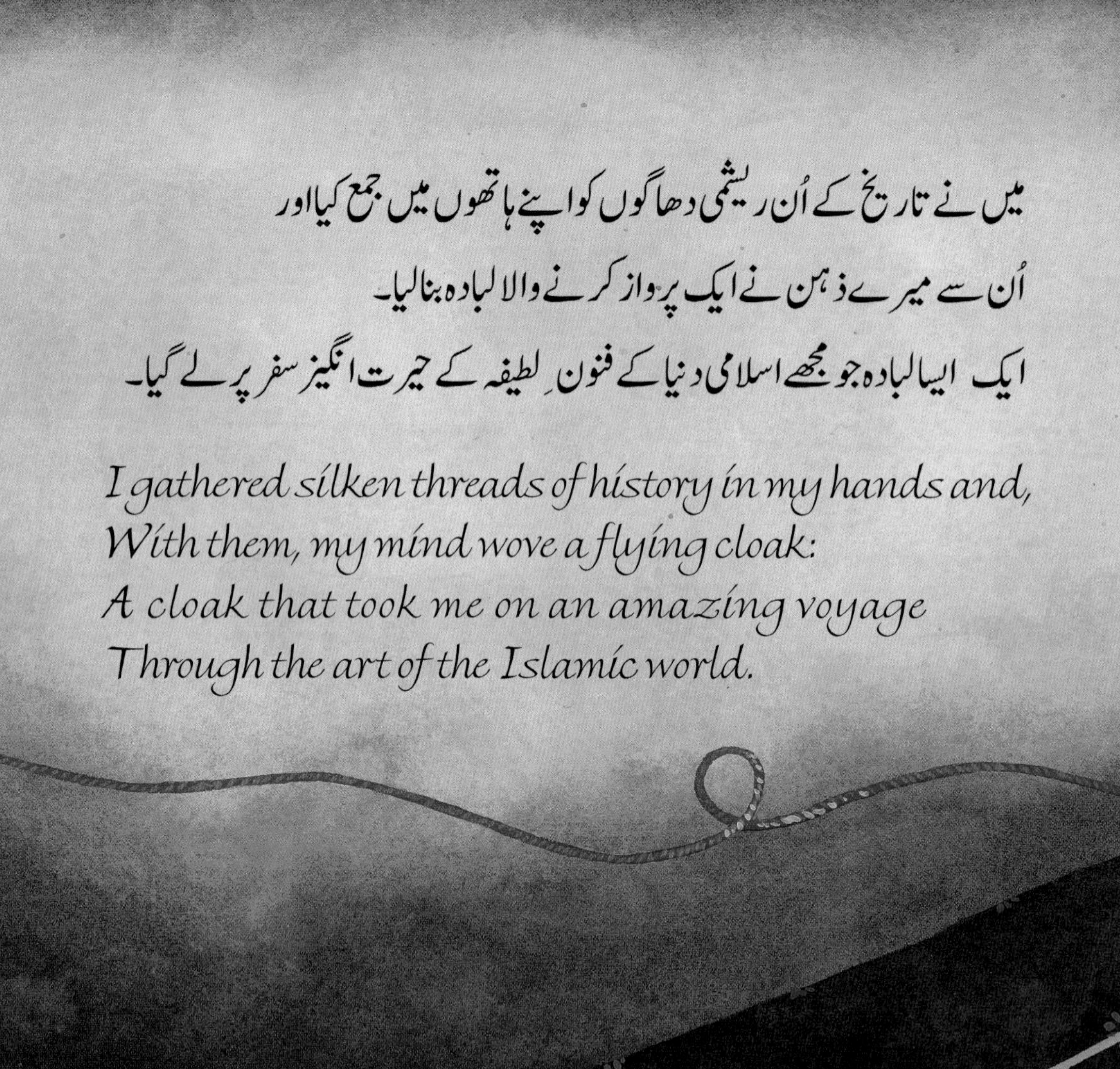

میں نے تاریخ کے اُن ریشمی دھاگوں کو اپنے ہاتھوں میں جمع کیا اور
اُن سے میرے ذہن نے ایک پرواز کرنے والا لبادہ بنالیا۔
ایک ایسا لبادہ جو مجھے اسلامی دنیا کے فنونِ لطیفہ کے حیرت انگیز سفر پر لے گیا۔

I gathered silken threads of history in my hands and,
With them, my mind wove a flying cloak:
A cloak that took me on an amazing voyage
Through the art of the Islamic world.

میرالبادہ مجھے بغداد کے قدیم شہر میں لے کر گیا جو مسجدوں، عوامی غسل خانوں،
گھڑدوڑ کے میدانوں، اور تفریح گاہوں میں بنی عمارتوں کا گھر ہے۔

My cloak took me to the old city of Baghdad,
Home to mosques, public baths,
racetracks, and pavilions.

جہاں ریگستان میں مورچہ بند مضبوط قلعے ہیں جو چھت سے فرش تک دیواروں
پر بنی مصوّری کے شاہکاروں سے سجے ہوئے ہیں۔
دنیا کی سب سے بڑی مسجد نے سمارا کو اپنا گھر مانا۔
مجھے ایسا محسوس ہوا کہ اذان کی آواز بادلوں سے ہوتی ہوئی مجھ تک پہنچ گئی ہے۔

Home to fortified desert castles,
Adorned with wall-paintings from floor to ceiling.
The largest mosque in the world called Samarra its home,
I imagined that the call to prayer reached me in the clouds.

میرا لبادہ مجھے مسلمانوں کے اسپین لے گیا جہاں مشرق اور مغرب کا ملاپ ہوا تھا۔
میں نے وہاں سے گزرتے ہوئے وہ سائنس دان، موجد اور شاہی علم فلکیات کے ماہر
دیکھے جو انسانی ذہن اور علم کو کسوٹی پر پرکھنے کی آخری حدود چھو رہے تھے۔

My cloak took me to Muslim Spain,
Where the East met the West.
I passed scientists, inventors and court astronomers,
Testing the limits of human knowledge.

وہاں میں سجے ہوئے صحنوں، فوارّوں، اور
خوشبوؤں سے لدے باغوں میں گھومتی رہی۔

There, I wandered through ornamental courtyards,
Past fountains and scented gardens.

اسلام اور اسپین کی تخلیقی اور
فنّی میراث نے ہم آہنگ
ہو کر الحمرا کا محل اور قرطبہ کی
شاندار مسجد تعمیر کی۔
گنبدوں، پتھر کے ٹکڑوں سے
آراستہ نمونوں اور راہداریوں نے
میری پُر شوق آنکھوں کو خوش آمدید کہا۔

The artistic heritage of
Islam and Spain
Fused to create the
Al Hambra palace and
the great mosque of
Cordoba.
Domes, mosaics and
archways greeted my
eager eyes.

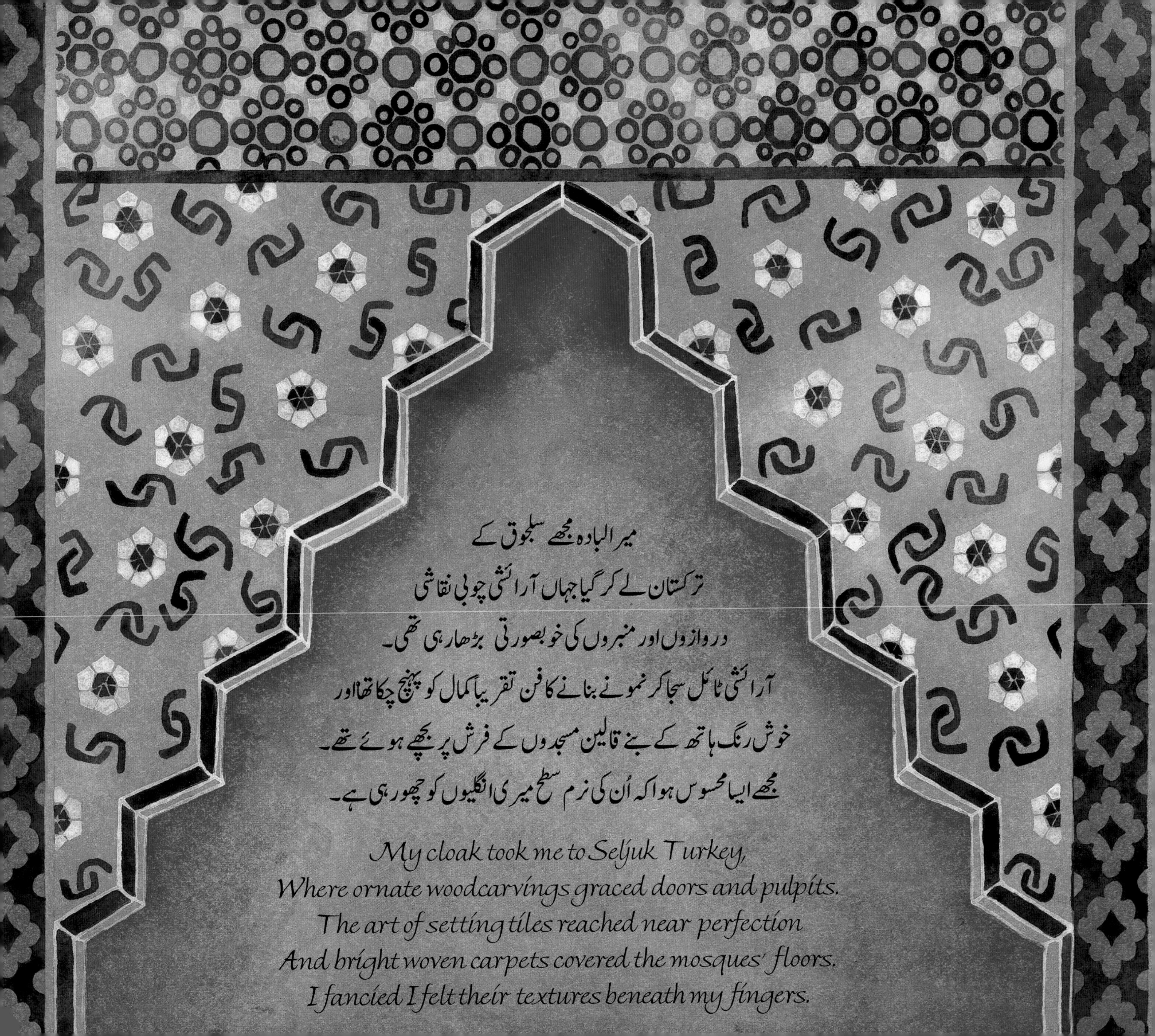
میرا لبادہ مجھے سلجوق کے
ترکستان لے کر گیا جہاں آرائشی چوبی نقاشی
دروازوں اور منبروں کی خوبصورتی بڑھا رہی تھی۔
آرائشی ٹائل سجا کر نمونے بنانے کا فن تقریباً کمال کو پہنچ چکا تھا اور
خوش رنگ ہاتھ کے بنے قالین مسجدوں کے فرش پر بچھے ہوئے تھے۔
مجھے ایسا محسوس ہوا کہ اُن کی نرم سطح میری انگلیوں کو چھو رہی ہے۔
My cloak took me to Seljuk Turkey,
Where ornate woodcarvings graced doors and pulpits.
The art of setting tiles reached near perfection
And bright woven carpets covered the mosques' floors.
I fancied I felt their textures beneath my fingers.

میرا لبادہ مجھے تیمور
لنگ کے سمرقند لے کر گیا جہاں تمام
دنیا کے ماہرینِ فن جمع کیۓ گیۓ تھے۔

My cloak took me to the Samarkand
of Tímur 'the Lame'
Where artisans from around the world
were gathered.

ہندوستان کے سنگتراش اور سنگساز،
ایران کے خطاطی کے ماہر،

Stonemasons from India,
calligraphers from Persia,

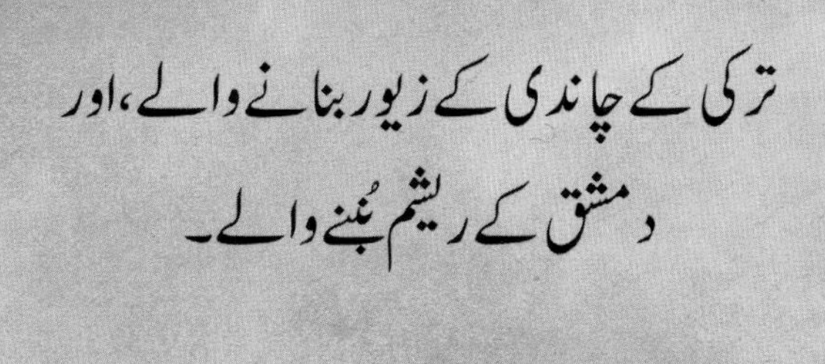

Silversmiths from Turkey and
silk-weavers from Damascus.

یہ سب لوگ قیدی بنا کر یہاں لائے گئے تھے تاکہ وہ اُس کے شہر کی خوبصورتی میں اضافہ کر سکیں۔
حالانکہ اُس کا اپنا محل صرف ایک خیمہ تھا۔ آخری وقت تک وہ تو خانہ بدوش ہی رہا۔

All brought back as captives, to beautify his city,
while his palace was a tent – a nomad to the end.

میرا لبادہ مجھے آگرہ کی سڑکوں پر لے گیا جہاں پُر رونق
بازاروں میں تاج محل کے متعلق قیاس آرائیوں کی دھوم مچی ہوئی تھی۔

My cloak took me to the streets of Agra,
Where rumours of the Taj Mahal filled buzzing bazaars.

ایک عمارت جو کسی کی آخری سانس کے ساتھ کیا ہوا وعدہ ہے۔
اُس کا سفید سنگِ مرمر کا لباس روشنی میں جگمگا رہا تھا۔

A building born from a deathbed promise,
Its garment of white marble
Shimmered in the light.

المشرق
قرآن شریف کی خوشخط لکھی ہوئی آیتیں
پھولوں اور پتیوں کی کندہ کاری کے نمونے،
مختلف شکلوں سے بنے آرائشی خاکے، سب ایک دوسرے سے ہم آہنگ تھے۔
اور شاعر نے اُس کو "صبح کا روشن چہرہ" کہہ کر مخاطب کیا تھا۔
میں نے تمنا کی کہ اُس کی خوبصورتی کسی کا مدفن ہونے
کی بجائے زندہ انسانوں کے رہنے کی جگہ ہوتی۔

Calligraphic inscriptions from the Qur'aan,
Floral arabesques and geometric designs
all harmonised
And the poets named her 'Dawn's bright face'.
I wished its beauty could grace the living
and not enshroud the dead.

یہ سفر محض ایک خواب تھا۔ ایک بچی کے تصوّر کی تخلیق۔
حالانکہ اِس سفر کی تمام منزلیں حقیقی ہیں۔
مجھے اُمید ہے کہ آپکا لبادہ بھی اِس قصّے کے تانے بانے سے بُن
جائے گا اور کبھی آپ بھی اُن مقامات پر جائیں گے۔

This voyage was a dream – a child's fantasy,
Though all its destinations are true.
I hope that your cloak will be spun by this tale
And that you will go there too.

Here are some explanations to help you enjoy the story:

Samarra
In the 9th century, after the foundation of Baghdad, the Caliph (ruler) moved his capital to the splendid city of Samarra. The Great Mosque was once the largest mosque in the Islamic world and rises to a height of 52 meters.

Islamic Spain was established in the 8th century by Muslims from North Africa who were known as Moors. For over three hundred years, Muslims, Christians and Jews lived together in a Golden Age when learning, art and culture flourished.

Seljuk Turkey was one of the eras in Islamic history. The Seljuks were Muslim rulers who took control of Persia and Turkey. Seljuk Turkey became the centre of excellence in weaving, ceramic painting and wood carving.

Born in the 14th century, **Timur 'the Lame'**, also known as Tamerlane, was a fierce and determined Mongol warrior who loved art. Whenever his armies invaded foreign cities, he would take care to protect the artisans and take them back to beautify his city, Samarkand.

The **Taj Mahal** was a monument built by the Mughal Emperor Shah Jahan in 1631 as a tribute to his loving wife Mumtaz Mahal. Legend says that she made him promise to build her a mausoleum more beautiful than any the world had ever seen.

Arabesque is an art form originally from Asia Minor. It was later adapted by Muslim artisans into a highly formalised form of intertwined flowers and plants.

The Qur'aan, the Muslim holy book, was revealed to the Prophet Muhammad (pbuh) by the Angel Gabriel. Its verses are often inscribed in beautiful patterns by calligraphers.

First published in 2005 by Mantra Lingua
Global House, 303 Ballards Lane, London N12 8NP
www.mantralingua.com

Urdu translation by Qamar Zamani

A CIP record for this book is available from the British Library.

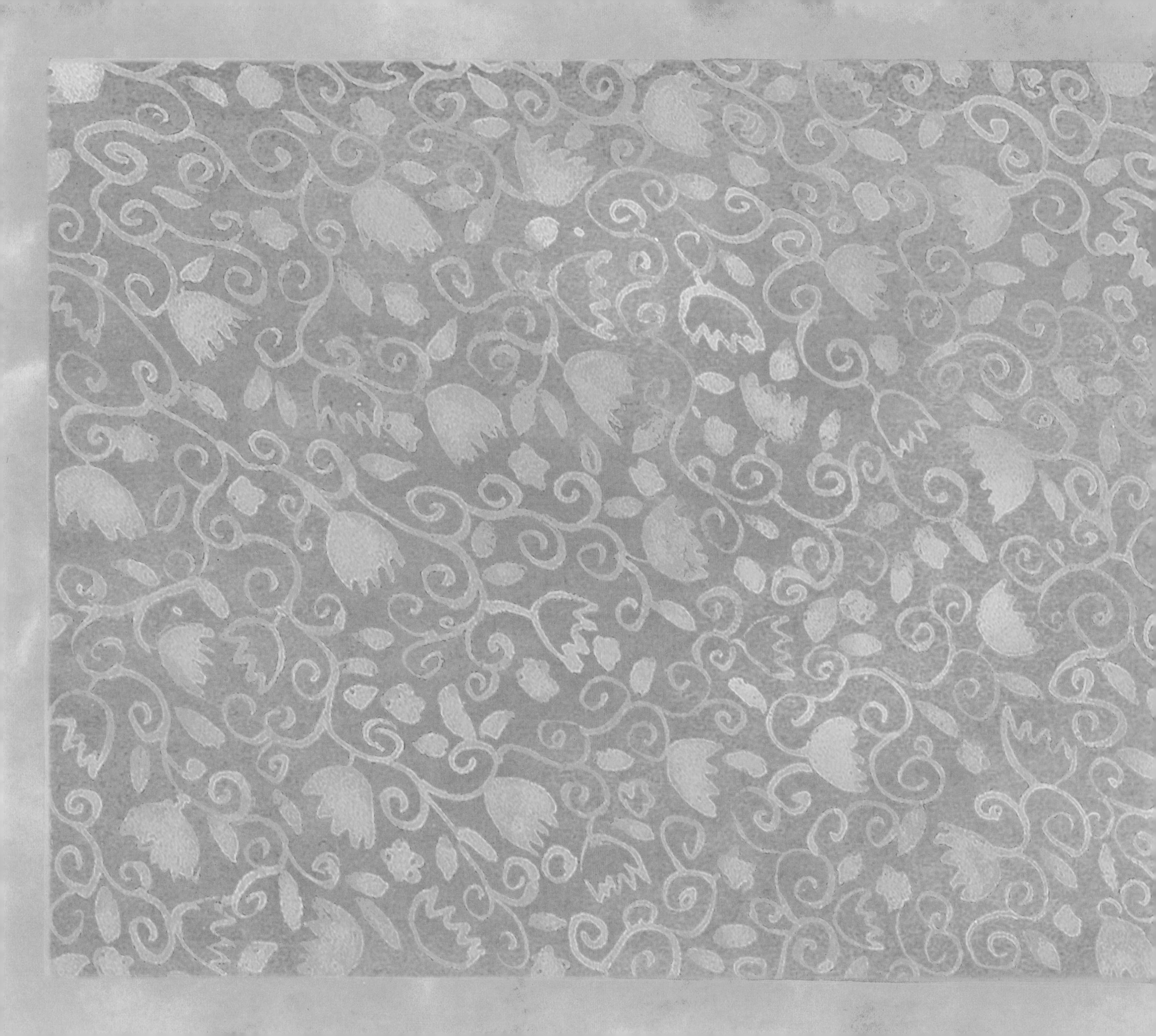